United States Marine Corps
Command and Staff College
Marine Corps University
2076 South Street
Marine Corps Combat Development Command
Quantico, Virginia 22134-5068

MASTER OF MILITARY STUDIES

SELF-INFLICTED WOUND
ALLIED DEFEAT IN CRETE, MAY 1941

SUBMITTED IN PARTIAL FULFILLMENT
OF THE REQUIREMENTS FOR THE DEGREE OF
MASTER OF MILITARY STUDIES

AUTHOR: Major Andrew J. Kostic

Academic Year 2001-2002

Mentor: Dr. John P. Cann
Approved: _____
Date: _____

Mentor: Lieutenant Colonel David A. Kelley
Approved: _____
Date: _____

REPORT DOCUMENTATION PAGE

Form Approved OMB No. 0704-0188

1. REPORT DATE (DD-MM-YYYY) 01-07-2002	2. REPORT TYPE Student research paper	3. DATES COVERED (FROM - TO) xx-xx-2001 to xx-xx-2002

4. TITLE AND SUBTITLE	5a. CONTRACT NUMBER
Self-Inflicted Wound Allied Defeat in Crete, May 1941 Unclassified	5b. GRANT NUMBER
	5c. PROGRAM ELEMENT NUMBER

6. AUTHOR(S)	5d. PROJECT NUMBER
Kostic, Andrew J. ;	5e. TASK NUMBER
	5f. WORK UNIT NUMBER

7. PERFORMING ORGANIZATION NAME AND ADDRESS USMC Command and Staff College Marine Corps University, MCCDC 2076 South Street Quantico, VA22134-5068	8. PERFORMING ORGANIZATION REPORT NUMBER

9. SPONSORING/MONITORING AGENCY NAME AND ADDRESS USMC Command and Staff College Marine Corps University 2076 South Street, MCCDC Quantico, VA22134-5068	10. SPONSOR/MONITOR'S ACRONYM(S)
	11. SPONSOR/MONITOR'S REPORT NUMBER(S)

12. DISTRIBUTION/AVAILABILITY STATEMENT
APUBLIC RELEASE
,

13. SUPPLEMENTARY NOTES

14. ABSTRACT
See report.

15. SUBJECT TERMS

16. SECURITY CLASSIFICATION OF:			17. LIMITATION OF ABSTRACT Public Release	18. NUMBER OF PAGES 60	19. NAME OF RESPONSIBLE PERSON EM114, (blank) lfenster@dtic.mil
a. REPORT Unclassified	b. ABSTRACT Unclassified	c. THIS PAGE Unclassified			19b. TELEPHONE NUMBER International Area Code Area Code Telephone Number 703767-9007 DSN 427-9007

Standard Form 298 (Rev. 8-98)
Prescribed by ANSI Std Z39.18

REPORT DOCUMENTATION PAGE		FORM APPROVED - - - OMB NO. 0704-0188

1. AGENCY USE ONLY (*LEAVE BLANK*)	2. REPORT DATE	3. REPORT TYPE AND DATES COVERED STUDENT RESEARCH PAPER

4. TITLE AND SUBTITLE SELF-INFLICTED WOUND: ALLIED DEFEAT IN CRETE, MAY 1941	5. FUNDING NUMBERS N/A

6. AUTHOR

MAJOR ANDREW J. KOSTIC

7. PERFORMING ORGANIZATION NAME(S) AND ADDRESS(ES) USMC COMMAND AND STAFF COLLEGE 2076 SOUTH STREET, MCCDC, QUANTICO, VA 22134-5068	8. PERFORMING ORGANIZATION REPORT NUMBER NONE

9. SPONSORING/MONITORING AGENCY NAME(S) AND ADDRESS(ES) SAME AS #7.	10. SPONSORING/MONITORING AGENCY REPORT NUMBER: NONE

11. SUPPLEMENTARY NOTES

NONE

12A. DISTRIBUTION/AVAILABILITY STATEMENT NO RESTRICTIONS	12B. DISTRIBUTION CODE N/A

ABSTRACT (*MAXIMUM 200 WORDS*)
EARLY IN WORLD WAR II GREAT BRITAIN AND GERMANY BOTH IDENTIFIED THE STRATEGIC IMPORTANCE OF THE ISLAND OF CRETE FOR CONDUCTING MILITARY OPERATIONS IN THE MEDITERRANEAN. THE ALLIES BEGAN DEFENDING CRETE IN NOVEMBER 1940 BUT ONLY COMMITTED LIMITED RESOURCES AND PERSONNEL UNTIL ALLIED INTELLIGENCE UNCOVERED THE DETAILS OF THE GERMAN INVASION PLAN FOR CRETE, OPERATION MERCURY. IN A LAST DITCH EFFORT, ALLIED FORCES EVACUATED FROM GREECE WERE SENT TO CRETE BRINGING THE NUMBER OF DEFENDERS TO 42,500 TO REPEL AN INACCURATELY ESTIMATED ENEMY ASSAULT OF 5,000 MEN. OPERATION MERCURY CALLED FOR GLIDERS AND PARATROOPS TO CONDUCT THE LARGEST AIRBORNE OPERATION TO DATE. THE PLAN PITTED 22,000 MEN AND 1280 AIRCRAFT AGAINST AN ERRONEOUSLY ESTIMATED ENEMY STRENGTH OF 5,000 MEN. THE DEFENDERS OUTNUMBERED THE ATTACKERS NEARLY 2 TO 1, KNEW THE INVASION PLAN, AND ESTABLISHED THEIR DEFENSE ACCORDINGLY. BY ALL ACCOUNTS, THE ALLIES SHOULD HAVE DEFEATED THE GERMANS AND IN FACT CAME QUITE CLOSE TO DOING SO. HOWEVER, FAILURES IN ALLIED LEADERSHIP AFFORDED THE GERMANS OPPORTUNITIES THAT THEY QUICKLY EXPLOITED. SUBSEQUENTLY, THEY WERE ABLE TO DEFEAT THE ALLIES WITHIN 12 DAYS. FAILURE IN ALLIED LEADERSHIP, NOT OVERWHELMING GERMAN COMBAT POWER, WAS RESPONSIBLE FOR THE ALLIED DEFEAT ON CRETE.

14. SUBJECT TERMS (KEY WORDS ON WHICH TO PERFORM SEARCH) CRETE, WORLD WAR II, LEADERSHIP, MERCURY	15. NUMBER OF PAGES: 52
	16. PRICE CODE: N/A

17. SECURITY CLASSIFICATION OF REPORT	18. SECURITY CLASSIFICATION OF THIS PAGE:	19. SECURITY CLASSIFICATION OF ABSTRACT	20. LIMITATION OF ABSTRACT
UNCLASSIFIED	UNCLASSIFIED	UNCLASSIFIED	

DISCLAIMER

THE OPINIONS AND CONCLUSIONS EXPRESSED HEREIN ARE THOSE OF THE INDIVIDUAL STUDENT AUTHOR AND DO NOT NECESSARILY REPRESENT THE VIEWS OF EITHER THE MARINE CORPS COMMAND AND STAFF COLLEGE OR ANY OTHER GOVERNMENTAL AGENCY. REFERENCES TO THIS STUDY SHOULD INCLUDE THE FOREGOING STATEMENT.

QUOTATION FROM, ABSTRACTION FROM, OR REPRODUCTION OF ALL OR ANY PART OF THIS DOCUMENT IS PERMITTED PROVIDED PROPER ACKNOWLEDGEMENT IS MADE.

EXECUTIVE SUMMARY

Title: Self-inflicted Wound: Allied Defeat in Crete, May 1941.

Author: Major Andrew J. Kostic, United States Marine Corps

Thesis: Leadership failures in the defense of Crete were essential factors contributing to Allied defeat on the island in May 1941.

Discussion: The Germans appeared unstoppable during the early stages of World War II. Inexperienced Allied forces were willing to fight, but the sentiment was the Germans were too powerful. Defeat became a forgone conclusion. To defend at all costs no longer appeared viable. Withdrawal and evacuation seemed almost commonplace in Allied strategy.

Great Britain and Germany identified early in the war the strategic importance of the island of Crete for conducting military operations in the Mediterranean. Operationally the British maintained naval supremacy in the Mediterranean, while the German Luftwaffe ruled the skies.

The Allies began defending Crete in November 1940. However, the Middle East Command put little effort into defending the island and changed Crete Force Commanders on a monthly basis. Allied intelligence uncovered the details of the German invasion plan for Crete. In a last ditch effort, forces evacuated from Greece were sent to Crete to bolster the defenses. This brought the total number of Allied defenders to 42,500 to repel an estimated enemy assault of 5,000 men.

The German plan for the occupation of Crete, Operation MERCURY, called for gliders and Hitler's elite paratroops to conduct the largest airborne operation to date. The plan pitted 22,000 men and 1280 aircraft against an erroneously estimated enemy strength of 5,000 men. The success of this plan relied upon surprise and the paratroops securing one of the three airfields on the island so reinforcements could be flown in.

A reluctant Crete Force Commander set the tone for subordinate commanders leadership failures. The invasion began the morning of 20 May 1941. The Germans suffered heavy casualties. At the end of the first day of fighting, they were short ammunition, and the Allies maintained control of the airfields. However, the battalion commander defending the airfield at Maleme, lacking communications and situational awareness, was unaware of the success of his unit and that night mistakenly ordered its withdrawal from the airfield. The Germans occupied the airfield in the morning and reinforcements were flown in. The Allies conducted an attack the night of 21 May to retake the airfield, but poor Allied leadership at the Brigade and Division level resulted in failure. Consequently, the Germans were able to mass combat power on the island and defeat the Allies.

Conclusion: The defenders outnumbered the attackers nearly 2 to 1, knew the invasion plan, and established their defense accordingly. By all accounts, the Allies should have defeated the Germans and in fact came quite close to doing so. However, failures in Allied leadership afforded the Germans opportunities that were quickly exploited. Subsequently, they were able to defeat the Allies within 12 days. Failure in Allied leadership, not overwhelming German combat power, was responsible for the Allied defeat on Crete.

PREFACE

There has been much written about the battle for Crete during May of 1941. Most of this literature focuses on the exploits of the elite German paratroops, how an airborne force defeated a numerically superior foe, and how German combat power was the deciding factor in the outcome of the battle. This paper explores another aspect relevant to the Allies' defeat on Crete—failure in Allied leadership. Allied leadership failures during the preparation of defenses, as well as during the first crucial days of the battle, where instrumental to the Allied defeat on Crete.

I would like to thank Sergeant Brenton Beach of the New Zealand Army and the New Zealand Army Museum in Waiouru, New Zealand, for providing cassette recordings of interviews with survivors of the battle and for providing official histories of units participating in the battle.

CONTENTS

LIST OF MAPS

SELF-INFLICTED WOUND

ALLIED DEFEAT IN CRETE, MAY 1941

A LANDMARK IN HISTORY

The island of Crete, cradle of civilization, is home to the Minoan culture, which flourished between 3000 and 1400 B.C. Ruins of the Minoan capital, Knossos, have been miraculously well preserved and tell of the importance of Crete in the ancient world. As long as there have been ships, Crete's position in the Mediterranean Sea has made the island strategically important. For centuries, civilizations have fought for control of Crete, the possession of which has usually coincided with the zenith of the controlling power.[1] This axiom would hold true in the twentieth century during the reign of The Third Reich.

Germany executed Operation MERCURY, the invasion of Crete, in May 1941. Like many battles fought during the Second World War, Operation MERCURY provided its own unique twist to warfare. Operation MERCURY was conceived as a joint operation consisting of the largest airborne invasion to date with follow-on support to be provided by seaborne forces.[2] The German General Staff had a mere 25 days from the time Hitler issued the order for Operation MERCURY until German airborne forces descended on the island. A logistical nightmare, the

---

[1] Daniel M. Davin, *Crete: Official History of New Zealand in the Second World War 1939 – 45* (London: Oxford University Press, 1953), 2.

German General Staff managed to pool an unprecedented amount of transport, bomber, and fighter aircraft to execute Operation MERCURY. Ships of various sorts were hastily assembled for the transport of heavy weapons, supplies and additional combat troops across the Aegean Sea. Assembling the forces of Hitler's "elite unit"—the paratroops—was in itself a challenge.[3]

Hitler's most prized fighting force was his paratroop unit. The paratroops were an elite unit, "the toughest fighters in the Wermacht."[4] They came from all corners of Germany and were the most athletic and adventurous men the country had to offer. Only one in four men desiring to join the paratroops could survive the rigorous training and meet the high standards required to receive the "sign of the plunging eagle," the coveted paratrooper badge.[5] The paratroops had proven themselves in combat during smaller airborne operations in Holland, Norway, Denmark and Belgium.

Allied intelligence reported German forces massing in the south of Greece for a suspected invasion of Crete. The Allies, in a desperate attempt to stop the wave of German victories, assembled whatever forces were on hand in the Mediterranean to make a stand on Crete. The Allies were given ample time to establish a defense, and the Allied High Command decided Crete would be the place where it would attempt to stop the German advance.

Allied intelligence prepared the defenders of Crete with detailed information regarding the German invasion plan, and they were prepared for the airborne forces on the morning of 20 May 1941 when the German Luftwaffe filled the skies over Crete with dive-bombers, fighters, gliders,

---

[2] Winston S. Churchill, *The Grand Alliance: The Second World War* (Boston: Houghton Mifflin Co., 1950), 284.

[3] Conrad Seibt, *The Crete Operation* (Europe: Historical Division, Headquarters, United States Army, n.d.), 7-10. Major General Seibt was the Supply and Administration Officer for the German paratroops for the Crete invasion. Seibt wrote this report for the U.S. Army upon the conclusion of World War II.

[4] Michael Veranov, ed., *The Third Reich at War* (New York: Galahad Books, 1999), 172.

[5] Baron von der Heydte, *Deadalus Returned: Crete 1941*, trans. W. Stanley Moss (London: Hutchinson & Co, 1958), 21. General von der Heydte was the Commanding Officer of the German 3d Parachute Regiment during the invasion of Crete; Callum MacDonald, *The Battle of Crete* (New York: McMillan, 1993), 16.

and parachutes. Courageous Allied soldiers went toe-to-toe with Hitler's elite paratroops and defeated their initial attacks. When the sun set on 20 May, the situation looked grim for the Germans: casualties were high, ammunition was low, and they had failed to achieve any of their objectives. However, during the course of the night, poor decisions by Allied leaders created opportunities that the Germans rapidly exploited. The momentum of the battle turned in favor of the Germans, and by the first day of June, they were able to declare victory on Crete.

The Germans' capture of Crete was a landmark in the history of war. "Never before had a country only accessible by the sea been overrun by a power not possessing even local naval superiority."[6] The Allied Commander-in-Chief of the Middle East reported after the battle, "The failure to hold Crete was due mainly to the overwhelming superiority of the enemy aircraft and the way in which it was handled in conjunction with ground troops."[7] German boldness and air supremacy indeed played a significant role in their success. However, as we shall see, Allied leadership failures in the defense of Crete were the most critical factors contributing to their defeat in May 1941.

---

[6] J.R.M. Butler, *Grand Strategy*, vol. 2 of *History of the Second World War: September 1939 – June 1941* (London: Her Majesty's Stationary Office, 1957), 515. Cited hereafter as Butler 2.

[7] Archibald P. Wavell, "Operations in the Middle East; 7 February 1941, to 15 July 1941," *Supplement to the London Gazett*, 3 July 1946, 3437.

OPERATION MERCURY

Strategic Value of Crete

By May 1941, the German war machine was in full gear wreaking death and destruction throughout Europe. Hitler won victory after victory and delivered crushing defeats to every foe he confronted. Italy invaded North Africa and Greece; and with the Germans aiding their endeavors, the Allies suffered devastating defeats. The Axis Powers threatened the Middle East and it appeared nothing could stop them. With Hitler's forces victorious in Greece, war was once again knocking at the door of Crete.

Crete is a Greek island centrally located in the eastern Mediterranean Sea. It is approximately 200 miles from both Athens, to the north, and the north coast of Africa, to the south. Alexandria is approximately 420 miles southeast of Crete and Malta is roughly 500 miles west. The strategic position of Crete in the Mediterranean made it an object of great desire by both the British and the Germans.

Mediterranean Sea

4

Crete is the fifth largest island in the Mediterranean and is approximately 160 miles long with a width ranging between 5 and 35 miles across. The terrain on Crete is extremely rugged. A backbone of barren mountains runs its entire length rising in places to over 8000 feet. Towards the northern coast the slopes are gradual, but to the south they are steep.

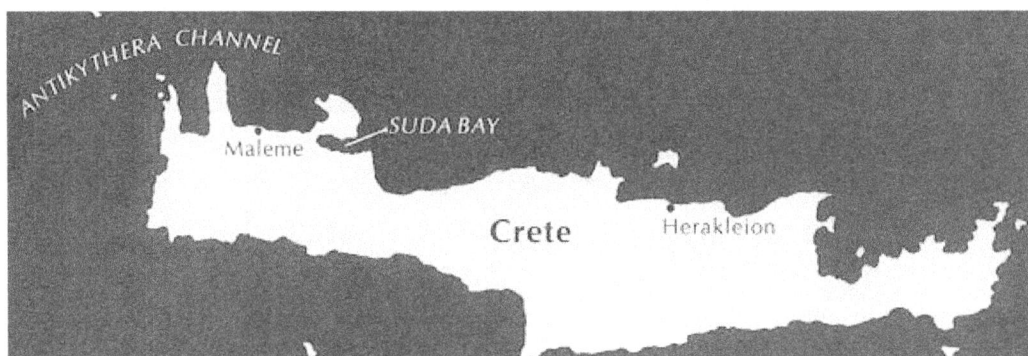

The Island of Crete

In 1941 the only port facilities fit for cargo vessels were on the north coast of Crete at Souda Bay and Heraklion. These ports were among the largest in the Mediterranean, although they required much work in order to handle more than a few modern warships at one time. There were no significant railways on Crete. Telegraphs, telephones, and transportation were all primitive. There was but one main road—in many places very bad—that ran along the north coast. It linked all the major towns and the islands three primitive airfields located at Maleme, Rethymnon, and Heraklion. There were very few roads connecting the northern coast to the southern coast. Those that did exist were extremely poor and most were nothing more than mule-paths that traversed the mountainous terrain.[8]

The British saw early on the strategic importance of Crete. Winston Churchill, in his directive of October 1940, stated, "One salient strategic fact leaped out upon us—CRETE. The

5

Italians must not have it. We must get it first and at once."[9] One reason for this was that maintaining the sea lines of communications through the Mediterranean was essential for the Allies to expeditiously supply the Russians, and the occupation of Crete would aid in this effort. Second, the fine anchorage at Souda Bay was ideally situated for a fueling base for the Royal Navy between the British ports of Alexandria and Malta.[10] Third, the airfield at Heraklion could be used as a refueling base for Royal Air Force (RAF) aircraft on their way from North Africa to Greece or for operations over the Aegean Sea and Dodecanese Islands. Fourth, bases on Crete would enable the British to continue attacks on Axis shipping to North Africa. Fifth, forces operating out of Crete would be better able to protect Egypt and Malta thereby making it possible to effectively counter operations by Italian air and naval forces at nearby Rhodes.[11]

Crete also possessed a strategic value for the Germans, primarily due to Hitler's desire to eliminate all possible threats to southeast Europe by British air or naval forces. To begin with, Hitler was concerned that during his war with the Soviet Union the Allies would conduct air attacks on the Romanian oilfields from bases on Crete. Next, the German Naval War Staff believed the possession of Crete was essential in order for the Axis Powers to drive the British out of the Mediterranean. In addition, Hitler's Luftwaffe operating from airfields on Crete would be able to paralyze British shipping through the Suez Canal. Finally, possessing Crete would be the best way to support General Erwin Rommel and the Italians in North Africa.[12]

---

[8] I.S.O. Playfair, *The Mediterranean and Middle East*, vol. 2 of *History of the Second World War: The Germans come to the Help of their Ally*, 2d imp. (London: Her Majesty's Stationary Office, 1961), 122-123. Cited hereafter as Playfair 2.

[9] Peter Singleton-Gates, *General Lord Freyberg, V.C.: An Unofficial Biography* (London: Michael Jospeph, 1963), 147.

[10] Playfair 2, 121.

[11] Gerhard Schreiber, ed., *The Mediterranean, South-east, and North Africa 1939 – 1941*, vol. 3 of *German and the Second World War: From Italy's declaration of non-belligerence to the entry of the United States into the war*, trans. Dean S. McMurry and others (New York: Oxford University Press, 1995), 531. Cited hereafter as Schreiber 3.

[12] Schreiber 3, 527-530.

Operational Situation

The operational situation in the Mediterranean gave both Britain and Germany distinct military advantages. Britain's maritime power permitted its Royal Navy to dominate the Italian Navy, while German naval presence in the Mediterranean was virtually non-existent. While the Allies possessed naval supremacy around Crete, Germany ruled the skies. Recent Axis victories in Greece gave Germany a semi-circle of aerodromes north of Crete with some as close as 60 miles. From these aerodromes, the Luftwaffe was able to gain and maintain air supremacy over Crete. RAF fighter aircraft operating at the limit of their range from Alexandria, over 400 miles away, were no match for the Luftwaffe. In the battle between air and sea, Germany's air supremacy triumphed over Britain's naval supremacy. British naval operations in and around Crete were restricted to fast ships operating during the hours of darkness.[13]

The Defense of Crete

British advance parties began arriving in Crete from Alexandria on 1 November 1940 and began Operation SCORCHER, the defense of Crete. By February 1941, at Churchill's urging, the three airfields on Crete were ready for use, and elements of the Mobile Naval Base Defense Organization (MNBDO)[14] along with additional coastal defense guns and air defense assets

---

[13] Schreiber 3, 510.

[14] The MNBDO was a Royal Marine unit designed to help build, defend, and operate fleet bases set up on short notice wherever required. It consisted of a landing and maintenance group to build docks, roads, and storage facilities; a defense group with coastal, anti-aircraft and searchlight batteries; and a land defense force including light artillery, machine guns, and riflemen. Only about one quarter of the organization, about 2200 men, were sent to Crete.

reinforced the defenses on Crete.[15] By May 1941, Allied forces on Crete totaled approximately 42,500 and were a conglomerate of soldiers, sailors, airmen, and marines from Great Britain, Australia, New Zealand, and Greece.[16]

The 2nd New Zealand Division, commanded by General Bernard C. Freyberg, was evacuated from Greece during the German push south, and arrived in Crete between 25 and 29 April. Freyberg was appointed Crete Force (Creforce) Commander on 30 April and was entrusted with command of all Allied forces on the island.[17]

British intelligence agencies, with the use of the ULTRA decryption system, erased any mystery of German intent in the Mediterranean. Through ULTRA, the British learned as early as 26 April of a large airborne assault intended for Crete.[18] Freyberg received a message from Middle East Command Headquarters on 6 May classified "Secret and Most Immediate" that revealed 17 May to be the date of the German invasion and listed details of the invasion plan.[19] ULTRA kept Freyberg abreast of German plans and adjustments in the invasion date, which initially changed from 17 to 19 May and then to 20 May. Consequently, he could relax his posture and conserve the energy of his forces by not having them on a constant state of high alert.[20]

With ULTRA information, Freyberg was able to align his defense to counter the German invasion plan. He was forced to divide his Creforce into four widely separated groups to defend four separate sectors of anticipated attack. It was clear that the long distance between these strong points, the shortage of transportation, and the inadequacy of communication assets would

---

[15] Davin, 6-7; Schreiber 3, 531-532. The total number of anti-aircraft guns on Crete was 32 Heavy and 36 Light.

[16] Davin, 480.

[17] Butler 2, 511.

[18] F.H. Hinsly, *British Intelligence in the Second World War* (New York: Cambridge University Press, 1993), 81.

[19] Hinsly, 83.

make it necessary for all four sectors to be semi-independent. On 30 April Freyberg issued Creforce Order Number (No.) 3 establishing this defense plan.[21] The defensive sectors and number of forces assigned were as follows: Chania and Souda Bay sector 15,227, Maleme sector 11,859, Central sector (Rethymnon and Georgeopolis) 6,730, and Heraklion sector 8,024.[22] Sector commanders were responsible for positioning forces in their sector and for their own reserve structure. Freyberg designated a New Zealand brigade in the Maleme sector as well as a British battalion in the Souda Bay sector as "Force Reserve."[23] However, the mountainous terrain and the primitive infrastructure of Crete negated any advantage the Allies may have had by possessing interior lines, as they could not move forces within their lines with any ease. Freyberg initially had RAF and Fleet Air Arm (FAA) fighters operating on Crete to aid in the defense of the island.[24] However, by 19 May the Luftwaffe had given them such a beating that the remaining seven fighters were ordered to Egypt to prevent their destruction.[25]

The German Invasion Plan

On 25 April 1941, Hitler issued Directive No. 28 authorizing Operation MERCURY. Hitler entrusted to Reich Marshall Hermann Goering the general direction of the operation. Goering tasked Luftwaffe Air Fleet IV, commanded by General Alexander Lohr and located in Vienna, with preparing and executing Operation MERCURY. The airborne and paratroop units of the XI Air Corps, commanded by General Kurt Student, were placed under Lohr's command. In addition, the fighter and bomber units of the VIII Air Corps, commanded by General Wolfram

---

[20] Hinsly, 83.
[21] Davin, 43.
[22] Davin, 480-484.
[23] Playfair 2, 127.
[24] FAA was British naval aviation.

Freiherr Richthofen, would assume the task of providing escorts. Operation MERCURY was unique in that a significant number of ground forces were used without the participation of the German Army High Command. In planning MERCURY, only Luftwaffe officers were involved in the details of how ground forces could most effectively be employed to rapidly reduce Crete.[26] Total German forces assigned for the invasion were approximately 22,000 men and 1,280 aircraft.[27]

For numerous reasons, the Germans lacked adequate intelligence regarding Allied disposition and strength on Crete. First, Germany did not have an "ULTRA" equivalent to decipher Allied messages. Second, German agents in Crete could not obtain a clear picture of Allied defenses due to Allied security measures and lack of cooperation from the Cretans. Finally, German aerial reconnaissance was ineffective due to the Allies relentless efforts at camouflage and at conducting immediate action drills.[28] The Air Fleet IV staff assumed the majority of Allied forces were situated around the Souda Bay, Chania, and Maleme areas, but the exact number was unknown. As late as 19 May, the Air Fleet staff believed the invading forces would encounter only an infantry division, reinforced with remnants of an expeditionary force, and some Greek units. Total Allied opposition was estimated at 5,000 men.[29]

Lohr decided on the scheme of maneuver for Operation MERCURY only after much debate amongst his generals. He divided Crete into three Groups focusing on the airfields: Group West contained Maleme airfield; Group Central contained Chania, Souda Bay, and Rethymnon airfield; and Group East contained Heraklion airfield. The element of surprise was critical for

---

[25] Butler 2, 512.
[26] Schreiber 3, 534.
[27] Schreiber 3, 536.
[28] Allied forces mastered the art of concealment amongst the rocky terrain and olive groves on Crete. Allied Commanders routinely flew over their positions to confirm their unit's efforts at camouflage. Immediate action drills were conducted against aerial observation. Whenever aircraft were heard or spotted Allied forces would hide from view of the aircraft and cease all movement.

the success of airborne operations. The airborne invasion would be a four-pronged attack executed in two waves. The first wave consisting of airborne and paratroop units would begin the assault early in the morning and occupy the area around Maleme and Chania. The second wave consisting of paratroop units would be dropped in the afternoon, on the same day, and would occupy the area around Rethymnon and Heraklion. The objective of the airborne assault was to secure the three airfields so reinforcements and supplies could be flown in, but this was only a limited answer to the logistic requirements. Consequently, Lohr's plan also called for shipborne reinforcements and supplies to be landed the same evening of the airborne assault under the cover of darkness with Italian navy protection.[30] Because of British naval supremacy and doubts about Italian naval capabilities, seaborne operations were considered problematic. The Luftwaffe generals, protecting their plan from Italian infection, determined from the start that it was absolutely essential to plan for fully supplying the German forces on Crete by air.[31]

The Battle

Softening-up attacks by VIII Air Corps bombers and fighters began on 14 May and occurred daily thereafter with emphasis placed on the three airfields.[32] Beginning at 0600 on 20 May, the VIII Air Corps concentrated its attacks on the Creforce units around Chania and Maleme. The attacks reached a savage intensity just before 0800.[33] Dust and smoke hung thickly over much of the area and as soon as the bombing subsided, gliders swooped down to the west of Maleme and

---

[29] Schreiber 3, 539.
[30] Schreiber 3, 535 & 537.
[31] Schreiber 3, 538.
[32] Playfair 2, 131.
[33] Playfair 2, 132, & Schreiber 3, 543.

on both sides of Chania. Shortly afterwards, the sky was full of parachutes.[34] Freyberg, who was having breakfast when the invasion started, saw the gliders overhead and the paratroops dropping. He commented in a calm voice, "They're dead on time."[35] The intelligence provided by ULTRA was indeed accurate.

The first wave of the German invasion was underway. The Assault Regiment, landing in gliders, was to secure the Maleme airfield while the 7th Air Division paratroops were to secure Chania. The invasion plan intended, for the most part, for the landings to occur where defending forces were not. By landing on each side of Maleme airfield, for example, the assault force would then conduct a converging attack to capture it. On the whole, this plan failed because German intelligence regarding Allied defenses was incomplete. Large numbers of paratroops descended on top of defenders and found—before they reached the ground—that the Allies were ready for them. The Assault Regiment with 10 men in each glider suffered particularly heavy losses. German forces landing near Allied positions were quickly defeated. Only where German forces landed well clear of Allied defenders were they able to assemble into units and cause anything more than temporary problems for the Allies.[36]

The key terrain near the airfield at Maleme was Point 107. Located south of the airfield, Point 107 was a 300-foot hill that dominated the airfield and the surrounding area. The 22 New Zealand Battalion, with Lieutenant Colonel Leslie W. Andrew commanding, occupied Point 107 and was tasked with the defense of the airfield. It was obvious to both the Allies and the Germans that whoever possessed Point 107 controlled the airfield. Actions on Point 107 would play a major role in the outcome of the battle for Crete.

---

[34] Schreiber 3, 543.
[35] Ronald Lewin, *Ultra Goes to War* (New York: McGraw Point Book Company, 1978), 157.
[36] Playfair 2, 131.

The second wave of the invasion force was comprised of two parachute regiments of the 7th Air Division. The VIII Air Corps began its preparatory bombing of targets around the airfields at Rethymnon and Heraklion during the afternoon of 20 May. However, this time when the preparatory bombardment stopped there was a long pause in the battle before the paratroops began to fall from the sky. Delays at the airfields in Greece caused by limited taxiways and enormous dust clouds on the runways from departing aircraft forced the second wave of paratroops to be late. As a result of this delay, the Allies had more time to react. Consequently, German casualties were higher in the second wave than those of the first.[37]

A key requirement of the German plan was to secure one of the three airfields so reinforcements could be flown in. Without more men and supplies, the German forces would only get progressively weaker, and in a battle of attrition the Allies would prevail. The key for Allied survival was thus to prevent the Germans from gaining control of the airfields. By the end of the first day of fighting, Allied strategy had been successful. The German attacks on the airfields at Rethymnon and Heraklion had been soundly repulsed, and these airfields remained firmly in Allied control.[38] At Maleme the New Zealanders had also been successful. Although the fighting was costly, the companies of 22 Battalion were in relatively good condition and were able to maintain control of the airfield. The only problem on Point 107 was that, incredibly, the commanding officer of the 22 Battalion was unaware of the success of his companies.[39]

During the bombing and fighting on 20 May, the telephone lines connecting the 22 Battalion Command Post (CP) with its companies had been cut. Andrew had communications with Brigade Headquarters and requested reinforcements, but he was unable to establish communication with his three forward companies controlling the airfield. Misinterpreting this

---

[37] Schreiber 3, 546.
[38] Playfair 2, 133.

lack of communication as a sign that his companies had been overrun, and not receiving immediate reinforcements from Brigade Headquarters, Andrew mistakenly ordered his battalion to withdraw from Point 107 on the evening of 20 May.[40]

The German attacks subsided with the setting of the sun on 20 May.[41] The three forward companies of 22 Battalion, still in their defensive positions around the airfield but with no communications between them, took advantage of the lull in battle to improve their positions and sent runners to re-establish liaison with the battalion headquarters and adjacent companies. The runners reached Point 107 where the battalion CP was previously located, but it had already been abandoned. The company commanders were in disbelief when they discovered that the remainder of the battalion had vacated the high ground to their rear leaving them isolated and vulnerable. For the companies to remain in position meant capture or death by German envelopment once daylight came. The company commanders had no viable option but to withdraw from their positions and attempt to locate Allied lines.[42]

During the early morning hours of 21 May, German forces occupied the abandoned positions around Maleme airfield and Point 107. The Allies could still cover the airfield with artillery and a limited amount of long-range machine gun fire, but German aircraft were now able to land with desperately needed ammunition and supplies. Student, located in Athens, ordered the remaining two paratroop companies to be dropped into Group West near Maleme to aid in securing the rest of the area around the airfield. Transport aircraft with 5 Mountain Division forces landed at

---

[39] Davin, 109-111.
[40] Davin, 99-114.
[41] German forces were not extensively trained in night operations and subsequently did not conduct offensive operations at night during the battle for Crete.
[42] Davin, 117-121.

Maleme under heavy Allied artillery and machine gun fire. At an enormous loss of life and aircraft, 5 Mountain Division had arrived on Crete and the tide of battle had now changed.[43]

Realizing the graveness of the situation, Freyberg ordered the New Zealand Division to counter-attack the night of 21 May to retake Maleme airfield.[44] Meanwhile, German forces became stronger with every aircraft that landed. By the time the Allies conducted the counter-attack, their efforts proved to be too little too late.[45] The counter-attack failed and the demoralized Allied troops abandoned their efforts to retake the airfield.[46]

The British naval forces had better success the night of 21 May. Once again, ULTRA had provided them with the German operation plan. Shortly after midnight, Royal Navy ships located an Axis convoy of approximately 25 ships carrying reinforcements and supplies bound for Crete. The British engaged the convoy, sank some of the ships, and forced the remainder to flee. True to German fears, the Italians were ineffective. Approximately 800 of some 2300 German troops were killed at sea and all of their weapons and equipment lost.[47] During the early morning hours of 22 May, the British fleet spotted a second Axis convoy 20 miles south of Melos. As the Royal Navy closed in for the kill, the German Luftwaffe appeared overhead and forced the British ships to give up their pursuit. It was however, not before the British had succeeded in diverting the Axis ships from their destination. The Royal Navy had succeeded in preventing Axis ships from reinforcing Crete with much needed men, weapons, and supplies.[48]

---

[43] Schreiber 3, 546-547.

[44] Playfair 2, 135.

[45] The New Zealand Division possessed additional resources but decided to counter-attack with only two battalions. The counter-attack was initially successful in the darkness, and the Allies made it all the way to the edge of the airfield. However, with daylight came the Luftwaffe. The Allies could not sustain the attack and were forced to retreat.

[46] Davin, 211-224.

[47] Schreiber 3, 547; Playfair 2, 137.

[48] Schreiber 3, 547.

With the Germans in possession of the airfield at Maleme, and thus reinforcement capable, it was only a matter of time before the German forces on Crete would be strong enough to defeat the Allies. General Julius Ringel, 5 Mountain Division Commander, took command of Group West and pushed towards the east. Ringel's objectives were to reach Souda Bay in order to cut British supply lines and to relieve the paratroops in Rethymnon and Heraklion, whose fate was still unknown.[49]

Freyberg informed his superiors in Cairo on 26 May that due to German air attacks and dwindling quantities of supplies, his forces had reached their culminating point. The next day Freyberg, with consent from Cairo, gave the order for Creforce to withdraw and prepare for evacuation. The survivors of the Maleme, Chania, and Souda sectors moved to the southern coast of Crete near Khora Sfakia and were evacuated by sea between 28 and 30 May.[50] The Germans pushed east so rapidly that the Allied forces at Rethymnon failed to get the order to withdraw south. On 30 May they were completely surrounded and forced to surrender. At Heraklion, Allied forces were evacuated by ship during the night of 28 May. The Allied evacuation of Crete ended 1 June with the Germans capturing approximately 9,000 Creforce soldiers and 1,000 Greeks.[51]

---

[49] Schreiber 3, 549.
[50] Schreiber 3, 550.
[51] Schreiber 3, 551.

ALLIED LEADERSHIP FAILURES

The Question

How could a numerically inferior German force, equipped with only small arms and light weapons, possessing virtually no knowledge of the defending force's strength or disposition, defeat a well fortified Allied force that had forehand knowledge of the attacker's plan? The answer to this question is sewn in the seeds of Allied leadership.

A War Correspondent on Crete wrote after the battle, "…a hundred extra field wireless sets could have saved Crete."[52] It is true that Allied communications on Crete were poor, however, communications for the invading German airborne forces, scattered across the island by the blowing wind, were even worse. In the fog and friction of war, information regarding enemy and friendly situations will be sketchy at best.[53] This is when intuition and moral courage bolstered by determination and conviction takes hold in commanders and drives them to produce victories under less than ideal situations on the battlefields. This type of driving leadership was lacking at several levels of Allied command during the defense of Crete.

Middle East Command Headquarters

Failure in Allied leadership during the defense of Crete begins at the Middle East Command Headquarters. Leadership failures at this level set the tone for the defenders on Crete and handicapped them in their efforts. There is no argument that the Commander-in-Chief of the

---

[52] Singleton-Gates, 159. Major G.S. Cox made this comment in an article he wrote for the *Evening Standard* after the war. Cox was a lieutenant on Crete during the battle and was tasked by Freyberg to produce a paper, called *The Crete News*, to boost the morale of the fighting men. He was only able to produce a couple editions of the paper before his printing press was destroyed in the bombing.

Middle East, General Archibald P. Wavell, was an extremely busy man. The Middle East Command Headquarters located in Cairo was responsible for four, and then five, fronts during late 1940 and early 1941. Under its command were inadequate armies from which wondrous victories were expected. The Middle East Command Headquarters constantly received instructions from London urging rapid action based on the political perspective, usually without regard to the perspective of the commander in theater. The Middle East Command Headquarters had an enormous task, but this does not justify the failure in their leadership to adequately prepare the defenses on Crete.[54]

Wavell reported the defense of Crete was his "particular preoccupation."[55] However, a quick overview of events surrounding the defense of the island prior to the German invasion clearly highlights two critical areas where the leadership of the Middle East Command Headquarters failed in its responsibilities. The first area was the grave neglect in constructing a strong defense on Crete during the six months prior to the invasion. The second area was the repeated changes in commanders responsible for defending Crete.[56] These leadership failures directly influenced the defenders on Crete and altered their ability to maintain control of the island.

Regarding its failure to prepare defenses, the Middle East Command Headquarters failed to take full advantage of time and to allocate adequate resources for the defense of Crete. Prime Minister Churchill as early as October 1940 had stressed the underlying strategic importance of Crete, and continued to do so to the Middle East Command. Nonetheless, the Middle East Command Headquarters regarded Crete as, "Just another little island."[57] Even after a meeting

---

[53] U.S. Marine Corps Doctrinal Publication (MCDP) 1, *Warfighting* (Washington DC: U.S. Marine Corps, 1997), 5-7. Cited hereafter as MCDP 1.
[54] Singleton-Gates, 180.
[55] Wavell, "Operations in the Middle East," 3433.
[56] Singleton-Gates, 180.
[57] Singleton-Gates, 149.

with Wavell on 11 February, the Prime Minister's statement, "At all costs Crete must be kept," continued to fall on deaf ears.[58] Consequently, the Middle East Command Headquarters failed to give the defense of Crete the attention it required.

Major General Francis De Guingand, a member of the Joint Planning Staff in Cairo, commented on the Middle East Command's efforts towards Crete, "I'm afraid our defense policy never had great drive behind it."[59] Lack of men and equipment were not justifiable rationale for the Middle East Command Headquarters failure to make early efforts to adequately defend Crete. For more than two months, no action was taken when ample resources were available within theater.[60] Two months of dedicated preparations would have greatly enhanced the defender's ability to withstand a German invasion. General Guingand went on to say, "Remembering the small margin between failure and success, as well as what was achieved in a last-minute endeavor to put the defense of Crete in order, I have a feeling that we might have defeated this first Axis attempt at capture."[61]

Part of the difficulties the forces on Crete had in establishing a formidable defense stemmed from the lack of resolve of the Middle East Command Headquarters to designate one commander to oversee the establishment of a defense from beginning to end. The Creforce Commander changed with each month that rapidly passed by, a total of six commanders in a six month period. Consequently, no one commander, or staff, was able to devise a thorough plan, set that plan in motion, and then see that plan through to its completion.[62] The lack of continuity in Creforce Commanders resulted in the delay of defensive endeavors and in operations on Crete taking a back seat to other efforts in theater.

---

[58] Davin, 7.
[59] Singleton-Gates, 150.
[60] Singleton-Gates, 150.
[61] Singleton-Gates, 150.

When Freyberg took command of Creforce on 30 April, he was its sixth commander within a six-month period.[63] He had to work with a defensive plan that five previous commanders had tinkered with but never completed. Instead of having six months to prepare a defense, he only had 20 days from the date he assumed command until the German invasion began.

Events up to this point in the war appear to have preconditioned the Middle East Command Headquarters to believe that the Germans could not be beaten. This would explain the lack of effort it put forth in the defense of Crete. Although Wavell was made aware of the vital strategic importance of Crete, he never committed to the belief that the Germans could be defeated. Wavell stated in a report to the Secretary of State for War after the battle, "…if we had been able to develop the defences [sic] of Crete more highly during the early period of occupation, we could have made the enemy's task in seizing it even more costly than it was."[64] Wavell never ascertained that defeating the Germans on Crete was within his grasp. He only wanted to make taking Crete costly for them. Surely this attitude influenced his decisions towards the defense of Crete, and perhaps it was this attitude that influenced the Middle East Command Headquarters to believe that Crete was just another little island.

Creforce Commander

Leadership failures among the forces on Crete begin with the Creforce Commander himself—General Bernard Cyril Freyberg. His leadership set the tone for subordinate commanders and was instrumental in leading the Allies down the path of defeat.

---

[62] Singleton-Gates, 149.
[63] Singleton-Gates, 149.
[64] Wavell, "Operations in the Middle East," 3434.

Freyberg was born 21 March 1889, in the town of Richmond, Surrey County, England. His family immigrated to Wellington, New Zealand, in 1891.[65] A rather large and athletic individual, he initially pursued a profession in dentistry for which he was mismatched in temperament and physique.[66] He stated to a friend in 1913, "I know there will be war soon and I'll die of a broken heart if I can't go."[67] In his longing for glory and fame, a situation not fulfilled in dentistry, he soon turned to the profession of arms. Events in Europe set the stage for the flamboyant and egocentric Freyberg to pursue his passion for glory and fame—World War I.

When war broke out in 1914, Freyberg applied for a junior officer position in a newly formed New Zealand Army unit, but the positions for junior officers in the new organization were already filled. With this disheartening news, he looked for an alternate way to fight in the war. He turned to the British to see if they would make him a junior officer in their armed forces.[68] Freyberg, possessing a strong background in aquatic sports, petitioned to the First Lord of the Admiralty, Winston Churchill, for a commission. Churchill was extremely impressed with the young Freyberg, commissioned him a lieutenant in the Royal Navy Volunteer Reserves, and assigned him as a sub-lieutenant in the Hood Battalion.[69] Freyberg's illustrious military career had begun.

Freyberg's courage and valor are not in question. During World War I he fought in Antwerp, Gallipoli, and France. He was wounded eight times and received the Victoria Cross for gallantry. He was again wounded in World War II and possessed some 30 scars from his

---

[65] Singleton-Gates, 17-18.
[66] Singleton-Gates, 20.
[67] Singleton-Gates, 27.
[68] Singleton-Gates, 27.
[69] Churchill, 272.

wounds, which he would proudly display if given the opportunity.[70] In addition to the Victoria

Cross, he received numerous other awards for valor.[71]

By 1941, Churchill and Freyberg had developed a special kind of relationship. Churchill was

in awe of Freyberg and had come to regard him as, "My heroic friend."[72] When Freyberg was

placed in Command of the 2nd New Zealand Division the Prime Minister had this to say, "No

man was more fitted to command the New Zealand Division," and, "Freyberg is so made that he

will fight for King and Country with an unconquerable heart anywhere he is ordered, and with

whatever forces he is given by superiors...."[73] Unfortunately, Freyberg would fail to live up to

Churchill's expectations on Crete. His cockiness, ego, and arrogance had deceived Churchill of

his true leadership potential.

Freyberg's first taste of battle in World War II was not what he had anticipated. Ever since

the New Zealand Division had departed Wellington, it had experienced nothing but frustration.

The defeat and withdrawal in Greece were not what the New Zealanders had expected. The

evacuation from Greece was chaotic and excruciatingly painful. The Division haphazardly

embarked aboard whatever ships were available and narrowly avoided capture by the Germans.

Once underway, Freyberg's primary concern was to return to Cairo and reassemble the Division.

Replacing casualties and organizing the Division back into a cohesive fighting force was

paramount in his mind.[74] In route to Cairo the ships carrying Freyberg and elements of the

Division anchored in Souda Bay. Some of the Division had preceded Freyberg and were already

---

[70] Singleton-Gates, 8.
[71] Davin, 25. Freyberg also received the following awards: Knight Grand Cross of the Order of St. Michael and St. George and of the Order of the Bath, Knight Commander of the British Empire, Distinguished Service Order with three bars, Order of Valor, and the Military Cross.
[72] Singleton-Gates, 9.
[73] Churchill, 272-273.
[74] Singleton-Gates, 145.

ashore. Freyberg and his staff went ashore to round up the New Zealanders and to arrange for their transportation to Egypt, his perceived destination. [75]

Freyberg believed his stay on Crete was only a temporary stop on the way to Egypt. [76] He had been on the island less than 36 hours when Wavell told him that he was to take command of the forces on Crete. Completely surprised Freyberg immediately responded, "I want to get back to Egypt to concentrate the Division and train and re-equip it." [77] Wavell had other officers capable of commanding Creforce and explained to Freyberg that Churchill had personally endorsed him for this command. Freyberg was dumbfounded and beside himself; he did not want this command. He informed Wavell that he would have to notify the New Zealand Prime Minister of this situation and stated, "My government would never agree to the Division being split permanently." [78] Wavell responded that he considered it Freyberg's duty to remain and take on the assignment of Creforce Commander. At this point, Freyberg could do nothing but accept. [79]

Freyberg was a man of limitations although his ego hid this from the public. Field Marshall Bernard Law Montgomery wrote in his memoirs, "Every officer has his 'ceiling' in rank, beyond which he should not be allowed to rise—particularly in war-time." [80] He concluded that a good divisional general does not necessarily make a good corps commander. [81] Freyberg's ceiling was command at the division level. He was at his peak in command of the New Zealand Division.

---

[75] Davin, 25.

[76] Davin, 24-25.

[77] Singleton-Gates, 146.

[78] On 29 April 1941 the New Zealand 6th Brigade accompanied Freyberg to Souda Bay. While Freyberg was ashore gathering other elements of the Division and arranging for transportation to Egypt, the 6th Brigade was transferred to transport ships and set sail to Alexandria.

[79] Singleton-Gates, 146.

[80] Bernard L. Montgomery, *The Memoirs of Field-Marshall the Viscount Montgomory of Alamein, K.G.* (Cleveland: The World Publishing Company, 1958), 79.

[81] Montgomery, 79.

When called upon to command larger forces he was never at his best and failed to live up to expectations, especially those of his friend Churchill.[82]

Freyberg was not enthused about his new command and found his situation somewhat depressing.[83] True to his word, he petitioned the New Zealand Prime Minister concerning the situation on Crete and his desire to proceed to Egypt. Freyberg recommended to his government that pressure be applied at the highest levels in London to either supply him with sufficient means to defend Crete or review the decision that Crete be held.[84] Any other officer taking this course of action would have been relieved instantly, and perhaps this is what Freyberg was hoping for. However, his special friendship with Churchill and the high regard the Prime Minister held for him prevented this from occurring. The British and New Zealand Prime Ministers discussed the situation on Crete. Churchill convinced his New Zealand counterpart of the importance of Crete in the overall defense of Egypt and of Freyberg being the right man for the job. Churchill also told his counterpart that additional resources had already been allocated for the defense of Crete.[85] Reluctantly, Freyberg accepted this decision and set about preparing the island for the impending invasion.

The defense of Crete would have been a difficult task for any commander, but to assign the task to one who openly rejected the responsibility and who went to great lengths to circumvent the command had all the makings of a tragedy. To his credit, Freyberg did a good job of concealing his true feelings from his soldiers. On 1 May he issued a special order of the day praising the Division's efforts during the evacuation from Greece, where "a smaller force held a

---

[82] W.G. Stevens, *Freyberg, V.C.: The Man, 1939-1945* (Sydney: A.H. & A.W. Reed, 1965), 117-118.
[83] Schreiber 3, 540.
[84] Singleton-Gates, 147.
[85] Churchill, 276.

much larger one at bay for over a month."[86] The special order bolstered the men's fighting morale by stating, "If he attacks us here on Crete, the enemy will be meeting our troops on even terms. I am confident that the forces at our disposal will be adequate to defeat any attack."[87] His ability to conceal his feelings from his men was evident in their determined and heroic fighting against the elite German forces. However, Freyberg could not hide his true feelings from the officers closest to him—the subordinate commanders of his own New Zealand Division.

Defeat was on Freyberg's mind from the start, and he wanted no part of it. Perhaps the Allied sentiment of the time is best summed up by a New Zealand platoon commander describing his feelings about being sent to Crete after being evacuated from Greece, "Nobody had beaten Hitler up to this stage and we just joined the rest of the group that had been beaten, but we were ready to fight."[88] Freyberg craved the honor of victory and the glory that goes with it, but his ego would not permit him to be associated with the responsibility of defeat. He was critical of Allied operations in Greece and the failure associated with it. In Greece he had played a small role in the grand scheme of things. His Division had performed well and avoided the stigma of defeat. Now he was in charge of all Allied forces and he did not believe the Germans could be defeated at this stage of the war. He immediately set to work insulating himself from any responsibility of the defeat he envisioned would occur by wiring the following message to Wavell:

> The forces at my disposal are totally inadequate to meet the attack envisaged. Unless the number of fighter aircraft is greatly increased and naval forces are made available to deal with a seaborne attack I cannot hope to hold out with land forces alone. The force here can and will fight, but cannot hope to repel invasion without full support from the Navy and Air Force. If these cannot be made available at once, I urge that the question of holding Crete should be reconsidered.[89]

---

[86] Davin, 42.
[87] Davin, 42.
[88] Haddon Donald, platoon commander, 22 Battalion, 2nd New Zealand Division, 1941, interview by Sergeant Brenton Beach, Army Museum, Waiouru, New Zealand, 18 August 2001, cassette 120 min.
[89] Churchill, 274.

This message was a calculated plan designed to accomplish two things: document his perceived shortage of resources and support for the defense of Crete; and shield Freyberg from the responsibility of defeat. Freyberg had more than 42,000 Allied forces under his command to repel the looming German invasion, which was estimated to be only 5,000 men. He had adequate forces and knew the Royal Navy was in support of his efforts. With this message Freyberg was setting the stage for shifting the responsibility of defeat from his shoulders to the shoulders of the Middle East Command.

Freyberg continued to set the stage for defeat and absolve himself of any responsibility for it. Taking advantage of his relationship with Churchill, he sent the Prime Minister the following telegram on 5 May: "When we get our equipment and transport, and with a few extra fighter aircraft, it should be possible to hold Crete. Meanwhile, there will be a period here during which we shall be vulnerable."[90] Freyberg was essentially telling Churchill that if the German invasion succeeded it was because he lacked the required support. One may ask if Freyberg thought Creforce was so deficient in resources, then why did he reject Wavell's offer on 7 May to send the 14th Infantry Brigade to Crete?[91] It was clear to the officers and men of the New Zealand 22 Battalion that if a few extra troops had been positioned on the west side of the Tavronitis River, the Allies could have held Crete.[92] During the evacuation of Greece the Allies left behind over 7,000 men to be captured by the Germans.[93] Perhaps Freyberg was already planning the evacuation of Crete and did not want to increase the number of forces he would have to leave behind.

---

[90] Churchill, 277.
[91] Singleton-Gates, 154.
[92] Donald interview; Frank N. Twigg, Intelligence Sergeant, 22 Battalion, 2nd New Zealand Division, 1941, interview by Sergeant Brenton Beach, Army Museum, Waiouru, New Zealand, 11 July 2001, cassette 120 min.
[93] Singleton-Gates, 142.

Despite reliable reports from ULTRA detailing the main effort for the invasion as airborne, Freyberg was convinced the Germans would conduct a large-scale amphibious landing. He sent a telegram to Wavell and Churchill on 16 May to highlight his unfounded fear of a seaborne attack and to once again set the stage for shifting the blame elsewhere. Churchill later commented, "He [Freyberg] did not readily believe the scale of air attack would be so gigantic. His fear was of [a] powerful organized invasion from the sea."[94] Churchill was confident that the Royal Navy could counter any seaborne attack, but despite his efforts, he was unable to convince Freyberg of this.

What rationale did Freyberg have for placing so much emphasis on a seaborne invasion? Perhaps this phobia stemmed from his experience in World War I. As a junior officer, Freyberg participated in the amphibious landing at Gallipoli. Although Gallipoli was an operational disaster for the Allies, Freyberg saw first hand the enormous amount of combat power that could be put ashore in a short period of time. Whatever the reason, his fear carried down to his subordinate commanders, and consequently, a significant amount of assets were positioned along the coastline instead of being placed around the airfields.

Freyberg did such a good job, prior to the invasion, of painting a bleak outcome for the defenders, that it came as no surprise to Wavell when he received the following cable on 26 May from his Creforce Commander:

> I regret to have to report that in my opinion the limit of endurance has been reached by the troops under my command here at Suda [sic] Bay. No matter what decision is taken by the Commanders-in-Chief from a military point of view, our position here is hopeless. A small ill-equipped and immobile force such as ours cannot stand up against the concentrated bombings that we have been faced with during the last seven days. The troops we have…are past any offensive action.[95]

---

94 Churchill, 277.
95 Churchill, 295.

27

The similarities between this telegram and the telegram Freyberg sent to Wavell earlier on 2 May is no coincidence. His self-fulfilling prophecy of defeat had come true, and just as planned, he did not see himself responsible for the defeat and neither did his superiors.

5 Brigade Commander

Another level of weak Allied command was the New Zealand 5 Brigade Commander— Brigadier James Hargest. Hargest's leadership failures had a direct impact on subordinate commanders defending the area around the airfield at Maleme. Specifically, his poor leadership resulted in control of the airfield being turned over to the Germans and failure of the Allies to retake the airfield.

The New Zealand 5 Brigade arrived on Crete on 26 April after its evacuation from Greece. The Brigade knew from the start that its stay on Crete would be more than just a brief stop over on the way to Egypt and that it would be participating in the defense of the island.[96] Hargest may not have been told how long his unit would remain on Crete but orders to him made it clear, "…Crete was vital to [Allied] operations in the Eastern Mediterranean and was to be held at all costs."[97] The 5 Brigade was immediately assigned the task of defending the Maleme sector, specifically to prevent the Germans from gaining control of the airfield.[98]

The 5 Brigade consisted of four battalions and a substantial engineer detachment with which to accomplish its task.[99] Hargest was well aware of the significance his brigade played in the defense of Crete. He fully understood the importance of preventing the Germans from

---

[96] Donald interview.
[97] Davin, 27.
[98] Davin, 57.

28

establishing a foothold around the airfield and stated in 5 Brigade Operation Instruction No. 4,

"In the event of the enemy making an airborne or seaborne attack on any part of the area, to

counter-attack and destroy him immediately."[100] Freyberg's fear of a seaborne attack carried

down to 5 Brigade and Hargest placed heavy emphasis on defending against it. Hargest had

ample forces to defend Maleme airfield; however, instead of concentrating his forces around the

airfield, he spread out his brigade to cover the nearly four miles of coastline between Maleme

and the town of Plantanias.[101] This tactical decision left two critical flaws in 5 Brigade's defense

that would prove detrimental during the battle.

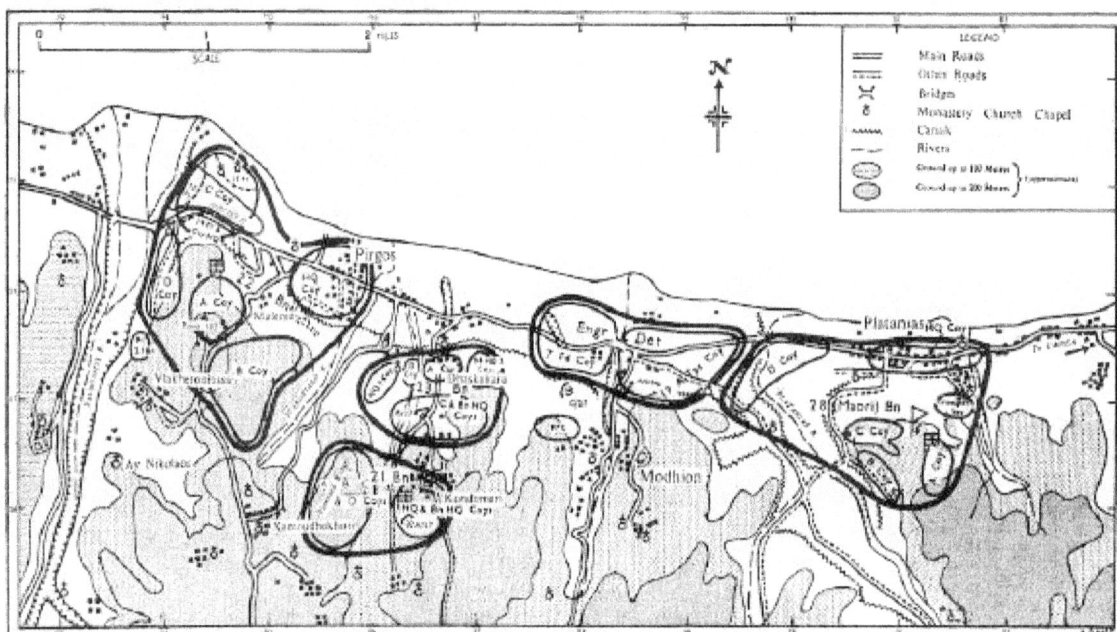

5 Brigade, Maleme, 20 May 1941

The first flaw was the failure to position forces on the west side of the Tavronitis River.

Hargest tasked 22 Battalion with defending the airfield and positioned his other three battalions

---

[99] The four battalions of 5 Brigade (21, 22, 23, and 28) were all in good condition and at approximately the same strength as they were before going to Greece with the exception of 21 Battalion. The 21 Battalion took significant casualties during the fighting in Greece and was reduced to approximately 250 personnel.

[100] Davin, 66.

[101] Davin, 77.

and engineer detachment to the east of the airfield. This lopsided defense proved effective in preventing the Germans from gaining control of the airfield from the east but afforded a clear avenue west of the Tavronitis River for the Germans to conduct a direct attack against the airfield. The only forces between the Germans amassing west of the river and the airfield were a few platoons from 22 Battalion. Had a battalion, or perhaps the brigade that Freyberg rejected from Wavell, been positioned on the west side of the river, the Germans would not have been able to take control of the airfield.[102]

The second flaw resided in the tasking of the brigade reserve force. Hargest designated 23 Battalion as brigade reserve. Anticipating the Germans' ability to make gains against the airfield, 23 Battalion was assigned the task of counter-attack force. Detailed coordination was conducted between the counter-attack force and 22 Battalion defending the airfield; however, the force Hargest designated as the brigade reserve, "to counter-attack and destroy the enemy immediately," had also been assigned a sector to defend.[103] Consequently, when 22 Battalion believed its ability to control the airfield was threatened and signaled for the brigade reserve to counter-attack, 23 Battalion was unable because it was engaged with enemy forces in its assigned sector.[104] The failure of the counter-attack force to come to the aid of 22 Battalion was a vital factor in the Germans gaining control of the airfield.

Hargest had other options besides assigning the brigade reserve a sector to defend. The 21 Battalion, although it had suffered significant casualties during the fighting in Greece, was capable of conducting a static defense mission.[105] This would have permitted 23 Battalion to

---

[102] Donald interview; Twigg interview.

[103] Davin, 66.

[104] Jim Henderson, *22 Battalion: Official History of New Zealand in the Second World War 1939-45* (Wellington NZ: Whitcombe and Tombs Ltd, 1958), 69.

[105] J.F. Cody, *21 Battalion: Official History of New Zealand in the Second World War 1939-45* (Wellington NZ: Whitcombe and Tombs Ltd, 1958), 80.

execute the counter-attack plan unimpeded. Even with these tactical failures 5 Brigade still had the capability to prevent the Germans from gaining control of the airfield, but Hargest's failures in leadership were too great for the brigade to overcome.

There were two significant periods during the battle for the airfield where Hargest's failures in leadership proved detrimental to Allied efforts. His actions were so blatant that his state of mind initially came into question. Hargest's leadership failures directly affected the Allies ability to maintain control of the airfield, which ultimately lead to their defeat.

The first period in which Hargest's leadership failures proved detrimental occurred the day of the invasion. Late in the afternoon on 20 May, the 22 Battalion Commander, Andrew, believed his battalion could not hold out much longer against the German attack which was pressing from the west. Believing the security of the airfield was in jeopardy, Andrew requested reinforcements. Hargest told Andrew that the counter-attack force was engaged and could not come to his aid. Hargest made no attempt to send other forces, in or out of the brigade, to reinforce Andrew. Maintaining control of the airfield was the brigade's mission, but instead of going forward himself to evaluate the situation and influence the battle, Hargest remained at Brigade Headquarters, approximately four miles away, and attempted to piece together what was going on through radio communications.[106]

Hargest failed to comprehend the direness of the situation and to understand his function as a leader to influence the actions of his subordinate commanders. With no reinforcements, Andrew believed his situation was hopeless. He radioed Hargest that he would have to withdraw and give up the terrain dominating the airfield. As vital as this terrain was for 5 Brigade to accomplish its mission, Hargest simply replied, "If you must, you must."[107] This response is

---

[106] Davin, 137.
[107] Davin, 110.

unpardonable for a commander. Hargest never attempted to bolster the flailing morale of Andrew or to re-emphasize the importance for Andrew to maintain his position at all costs. There were no words of encouragement from Hargest to hold on a little bit longer or to reassure Andrew that help was on the way. Instead of influencing the battle, Hargest sat at Brigade Headquarters and permitted the airfield to be handed over to the Germans.

Failures in Hargest's leadership continued throughout the evening. Although he had forces at his disposal that were not engaged, he never ordered a counter-attack. He eventually radioed Andrew that two companies were being sent forward to reinforce 22 Battalion, but Andrew had already concluded that withdrawing was the only option. Oddly enough, Hargest never ordered Andrew to retake the key terrain he vacated, and when the reinforcements arrived, Andrew continued his withdrawal. Andrew arrived at Brigade Headquarters late that night to find Hargest asleep in his pajamas. There is no doubt Hargest was aware that the airfield had been vacated; still he made no effort to initiate a counter-attack.[108]

The second period where Hargest's leadership inadequacies proved detrimental to success occurred during the evening of 21 May and extended to the afternoon of 22 May. Division Headquarters, upon discovering the airfield had been abandoned, immediately ordered 5 Brigade to counter-attack and retake control of it. Hargest, however, convinced the division commander that a daylight attack was too dangerous and requested permission to wait until darkness before beginning the attack. The importance of the success of the counter-attack was clear. Although additional forces were made available to Hargest, he only requested one additional battalion from division to aid in his two-battalion counter-attack.[109]

---

[108] Henderson, 71.
[109] Davin, 212-215.

The counter-attack was to begin at approximately 0100 on 22 May; however, Hargest failed to communicate to subordinate commanders the criticality of the time line for success and failed to ensure thorough coordination was performed in support of the counter-attack. As a result, the counter-attack was not initiated until 0330.[110] Hargest was perturbed by the delay, and became doubtful whether the attack should take place at all with dawn just a few hours away and the Luftwaffe coming with it. He contacted Division Headquarters and asked, "Must the attack go on?" Division replied, "It must." On it went—too late.[111]

Hargest's leadership failures continued to mount. He permitted subordinate commanders to execute the counter-attack, while he remained behind at Brigade Headquarters. Despite the late start, the counter-attack made good progress and was able to reach the outskirts of the airfield. However, by this time the sun was fully up and so were the Luftwaffe. Casualties quickly mounted, and the counter-attack came to a halt. Hargest, with poor communications, was once again unable to influence the fight.[112] At about noon on 22 May, the commanders on the scene, with no inspiration from Hargest, believed without adequate artillery and air support the counter-attack could go no further. Unable to obtain the additional support, the decision to abort the attack became the only alternative. The counter-attack forces withdrew over terrain they had fought so hard to gain just hours before. The attack had failed and with it the hope of defeating the Germans.[113]

Hargest's leadership failures were evident to his seniors. Colonel Keith L. Stewart, Freyberg's General Staff Officer, wrote afterwards, "During the vital first and second days and nights both or either 23 and 28 battalions in 5 Brigade sector could have been used to counter-

_____

[110] Davin, 193-196.
[111] Singleton-Gates, 166-167.
[112] Davin, 194.
[113] Davin, 224-225.

attack in the Maleme area."[114] By themselves, Hargest's inadequacies as a leader may not appear so significant. However, the impact of Hargest's leadership failures was magnified during the first crucial days of the battle by the leadership failures of subordinate commanders, specifically those of the 22 Battalion Commander.

22 New Zealand Battalion

Perhaps the most blatant failure in leadership detrimental to the defense of Crete rests with the Commanding Officer of 22 Battalion, Lieutenant Colonel Leslie W. Andrew. Poor decisions made by this officer on the evening of the first day of battle gave the Germans the ability to mass and sustain enough combat power on the island to overthrow the defenders. His actions changed the course of the battle and directly contributed to the ultimate defeat of the Allies.

Andrew's courage and bravery are not in question. He distinguished himself during the First World War as a regular soldier in the New Zealand Wellington Regiment. As a corporal, he won the Victoria Cross for bravery under fire while leading his section against numerous machine gun positions during a battle in France. He also received the Distinguished Service Order for gallantry in action. [115] However, physical courage is only one trait of being a leader, and not all courageous individuals have proven to be sound leaders.

The 22 Battalion was one of four battalions in the New Zealand 5 Brigade. Andrew and the battalion arrived on Crete on 26 April after being evacuated from Greece. He was given the primary task of defending the airfield at Maleme and its approaches. [116] The strength of 22 Battalion was approximately 20 officers and 600 men. It consisted of a battalion headquarters

---

[114] Singleton-Gates, 162.
[115] Davin, 55.
[116] Davin, 66.

section and five rifle companies: A, B, C, D, and Headquarters (HQ).[117] The key piece of terrain that Andrew anchored his static defense to was Point 107.

Andrew was briefed to expect an airborne invasion. Thanks to a previously captured German Airborne Operations Manual, the Allies knew how an airborne attack would unfold. They knew the size and types of units in the airborne organization along with the weapons, equipment and supplies that would accompany them.[118] To accomplish his task, Andrew positioned C Company on the airfield itself, D Company just east of the Tavronits River to defend the western approach, and HQ Company near the town of Pirgos to defend the eastern approach. To compensate for German airborne tactics, Andrew established a defense in depth by positioning A Company on top of Point 107, behind the three forward companies, and B Company on the ridgeline behind A Company. This would allow the defenders to engage airborne forces landing behind and between company positions.[119]

---

[117] Headquarters Company was trained, equipped, and fought as a rifle company.

[118] John Westwood, "Student and the Capture of Crete," in *Strategy and Tactics of the Great Commanders of World War II and Their Battles* (Greenwich, CT: Brompton Books Corp., 1990), 46.

[119] Davin, 53-54.

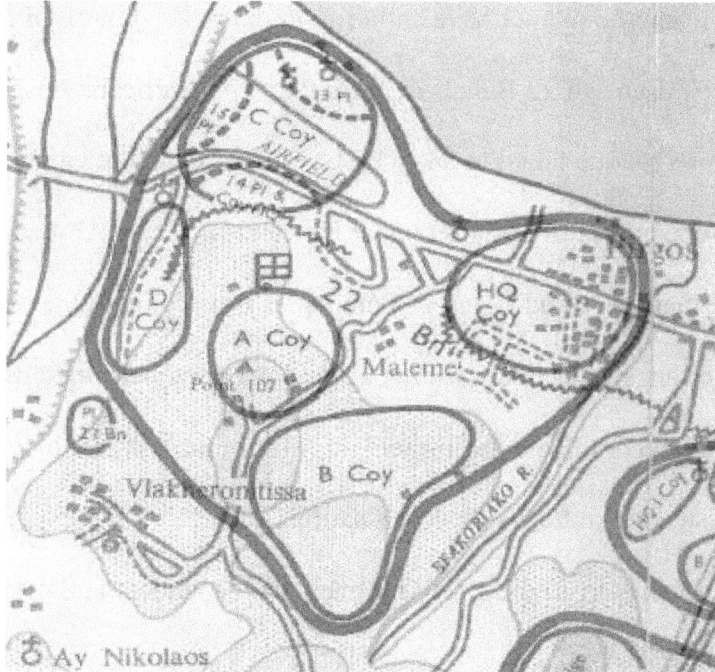

22 Battalion, Maleme, 20 May 1941

The entire Battalion was aware of the significant nature of the situation. They knew the airfield must be held at all costs to prevent the Germans from capturing the island. They anticipated the attack on Maleme to be more intense as it was the closest airfield to the Greek mainland.[120] In preparation for the invasion, Andrew conducted an aerial reconnaissance of the battalion's position to view the effectiveness of its camouflage. He coordinated with 23 Battalion, the designated counter-attack force, on the signal to initiate such an attack should normal communications fail, and confirmed the routes for 23 Battalion to execute the counter-attack.[121] He also informed his superiors of the lack of unified command in his area of operation (AO) where about 370 British and Australian airmen, soldiers and marines operated and

---

[120] Donald interview.
[121] Davin, 62-64.

36

defended the airfield whom he did not have authority to direct.[122] For all of Andrew's efforts to

improve the defensive posture of 22 Battalion, there are two significant areas in which he failed.

One of his faults was that he failed to take charge of his AO and integrate his defensive plan

with the other forces operating there but not under his control. The RAF had a tent camp near

the Tavronitis Bridge that prevented C and D Companies from tying in their defensive lines.

Even when aircraft no longer operated from the airfield, Andrew permitted the RAF camp to

remain. Andrew failed to coordinate the airmen's intentions or abilities to defend this area. As a

result, a huge gap existed in Andrew's defense that the Germans would exploit during the

attack.[123] The British forces in Andrew's AO remained independent and even had different

passwords among the groups.[124]

The other area where Andrew failed was planning and coordinating counter-attack operations

with forces organic to his battalion. Andrew was given two infantry (I) tanks several days before

the invasion. He hid them near the airfield in the event a counter-attack was necessary but never

coordinated their use within the battalion. In addition, he never planned for the use of A or B

Companies, positioned well behind the main defensive line, to reinforce the forward companies

or to be used as a counter-attack force.[125] These failures would haunt Andrew during the first

day of the invasion and would have a grave impact on the outcome of the battle.

Communications within 22 Battalion also played a role in the outcome of the battle and

influenced Andrew's decisions. Andrew positioned his CP just north of the high ground on Point

107 in A Company's sector.[126] Radios were issued down to the company level, but they were of

---

[122] Henderson, 48; Davin, 55. Australian Anti-Aircraft gunners defending the airfield were controlled from the gun operation room in Chania, MNBDO gunners were responsible to General E.C. Weston in Chania, and the RAF and FAA were under control of their own senior commanders.
[123] Twiggs interview.
[124] Henderson, 48.
[125] Donald interview.
[126] Davin, 98.

poor quality and did not work. The primary means of communication between Andrew and his company commanders were field phones. The ground was extremely rocky and entrenching tools were few. A majority of the wires connecting the field phones lay on top of the ground or buried just below the surface.[127] The pre-invasion bombing cut a majority of the wires, and paratroops, trained to sever enemy command and control, took care of the rest. As a result, communications between Andrew and his forward companies were severely impeded.

When the invasion began, 22 Battalion's battle almost immediately fragmented into a number of small separate battles. Andrew found it more and more difficult to operate his battalion as a unit.[128] He was able to maintain radio communications with Brigade Headquarters but lost phone communications with C, D, and HQ Companies. He resorted to using runners to obtain information on the status of these companies. However, using runners had only limited success, and German snipers made this method of communicating costly. Andrew quickly lost situational awareness and instead of fighting his battalion as a unit, he inadvertently turned the important task of defending the airfield into independent company actions.[129]

The invading Germans landed throughout 22 Battalion's area. Companies A and B quickly defeated the isolated pockets of Germans in their areas, suffered only minimal casualties, and saw little action for the remainder of the day. Andrew's close proximity to these two companies permitted good communications with them throughout the day. Companies C, D, and HQ took the brunt of the invasion with the German forces converging on their positions.[130] At 1055, Andrew sent a message to Brigade HQ estimating 400 paratroops had landed in his area. He also reported he had lost communications with HQ Company at the start of the invasion and

---

[127] Donald interview.
[128] Davin, 99.
[129] Davin, 110.
[130] Twiggs interview.

requested that 23 Battalion attempt to contact his eastern most company to find out its status. However, neither 23 Battalion nor Brigade Headquarters ever reported making contact with HQ Company. As the day progressed with no word from HQ Company, Andrew mistakenly believed the company had been wiped out.[131]

Andrew lost all communications with D Company shortly after midday; however, he reported to Brigade Headquarters at 1550 that he felt the situation was still in hand, but there was an indication of growing anxiety. Andrew's failure to coordinate and integrate defensive efforts in his AO soon came into play. German forces near the Tavronitis River found the gap between C and D Companies' lines—the RAF camp—and quickly pushed through it. The airmen, not trained as infantrymen, fled from their camp and passed near the Battalion CP in their flight from the Germans. Seeing these airmen franticly fleeing and listening to reports from wounded New Zealanders making their way to the aid station, Andrew mistakenly believed that D Company had also been wiped out. German mortar fire began coming from the RAF camp and forced him to move his CP 200 meters southwest just inside of B Company's area. Sometime after 1600 Andrew gave the prearranged signal for 23 Battalion to counter-attack, but no help came. At 1700 Andrew radioed Brigade Headquarters requesting 23 Battalion to counter-attack but was informed 23 Battalion was engaged and could not aid Andrew's situation. [132]

The second area in which Andrew failed during the preparation for invasion was now going to have a disastrous effect upon the defenders. Andrew ordered a counter-attack with the two I tanks and one platoon from C Company. He intended to drive the enemy from the western end of the airfield. Unfortunately, the only plan 22 Battalion had established for a counter-attack involved 23 Battalion, not the two I tanks. The counter-attack with the I tanks was not well

---

[131] Davin, 108.
[132] Davin, 108-109.

thought out, coordinated, or rehearsed. No. 14 Platoon Commander, Lieutenant Hadden V. Donald, first learned of his platoon's involvement in the counter-attack when he heard the tanks come rumbling down the road. He never had the opportunity to talk with the tank commanders let alone coordinate a counter-attack with them. There was no time for Donald to educate his platoon on how it would protect the tanks. He told his section leaders to pick up and follow the tanks. He then gave instructions to his platoon, "First section on the far side of the road, second section on the other side of the road, and third section near the road," as they tried to catch up to the tanks. With no prior planning, coordination, or rehearsals, the situation was hopeless and doomed for failure before it had begun. Before the platoons could catch up with the lead tank, it became bogged down near the Tavronitis Bridge, and the crew was forced to surrender. The second tank was then hit with an anti-tank shell. With the turret inoperable, the tank withdrew back the way it had come. The counter-attack had failed miserably and nearly every man in No. 14 Platoon was either wounded or killed.[133]

At this point in the battle Andrew believed the situation was hopeless. At approximately 1800, with the failure of the I tank counter-attack and no sign of 23 Battalion, Andrew informed Hargest that he would have to withdraw. As vital a mission as holding on to the airfield was to the defense of Crete, Hargest simply replied, "If you must, you must."[134] Hargest's solemn reply solidified Andrew's decision to withdraw. A short time later, Hargest sent word to Andrew that he was sending two companies forward to support him. However, Andrew's mind was made up and three and a half hours later, with darkness upon him and no sign of reinforcements, he gave

---

[133] Donald interview.
[134] Davin, 110.

the order for his battalion to pull back to B Company's position, approximately one half mile southeast of Point 107.[135]

Andrew stated that he initially planned to conduct only a limited withdrawal to B Company ridge. He apparently believed that by leaving a combat outpost on Point 107 he would be able to retain possession of the terrain overlooking the airfield. However, upon relocating to B Company ridge, Andrew realized his new position was extremely vulnerable to the dominating terrain of Point 107, which he had just vacated. He concluded that the combat outpost remaining on Point 107 would be no match for the concentrated German attack that he believed was sure to come with daylight. With the Germans on Point 107, Andrew believed that the remainder of his battalion on B Company ridge would be slaughtered.[136]

Why Andrew did not come to this conclusion prior to withdrawing from Point 107 remains a mystery. He had been to B Company ridge prior to the invasion and was very familiar with the terrain. He knew the all around tactical advantage of Point 107—which is why he chose it to defend initially. One hypothesis is that Andrew never really intended to conduct only a limited withdrawal and that a complete withdrawal from the area was his original intention. This theory is supported by the fact that while Andrew was on B Company ridge one of the reinforcing companies sent by Brigade Headquarters arrived. Andrew had plenty of time and a fresh company, along with A and B Companies, to strengthen the combat outpost on Point 107, but he chose not to do this. Instead, he ordered 22 Battalion to withdraw even farther from the airfield back to 23 Battalion's position.[137]

---

[135] Davin, 110-112. Andrew sent runners with the order to withdrawal to all five of his companies, but the runners were unable to get through to C, D, or HQ Companies.
[136] Davin, 112-114.
[137] Davin, 108-112.

41

Well after midnight the commanders of C, D, and HQ Companies, during their attempt to establish communications with the Battalion CP, discovered that the rest of the battalion had withdrawn and left them isolated and vulnerable to a German envelopment. They were furious! The three companies—at a high cost of life—had won a brutal day of fighting and still maintained firm control of their positions around the airfield. The company commanders knew that to withdraw meant the Germans would take control of the airfield, and then it would then be only a matter of time before they would take control of the entire island.[138] With no idea of the location of the rest of the battalion or of the battalion commander, the company commanders had no choice and reluctantly left their positions to try and locate friendly lines before sunrise, which was just a few hours away.

Andrew's decision to withdraw 22 Battalion from Maleme on the first night of battle would ultimately lead to Allied defeat. The first phase of the battle for Maleme ended not with a decisive battle, but with Andrew voluntarily giving up the airfield and withdrawing to 23 Battalion's position. For the Allies the tide had turned. It was now a question of recovering vital positions instead of keeping them, of attempting difficult counter-attacks instead of holding on in prepared defensive positions. With the loss of communications and the failure of the counter-attack plan, Andrew mistakenly believed 22 Battalion would not be able to repulse a German attack in the morning. It is clear that Andrew knew the value of Maleme airfield and the important role it played in the Allies ability to defend Crete.[139] Yet one cannot help but wonder if when Andrew made his decision to withdraw was he thinking about his critical mission to defend the airfield, its vital importance to the defense of Crete, and the commander's guidance to hold Crete at all costs, or was he thinking about the defeat he experienced in Greece just a few

---

[138] Davin, 111-119.
[139] Donald interview.

42

short weeks earlier, the withdrawal and the subsequent evacuation which by now must have seemed almost commonplace in Allied strategy?

The situation was not as bleak as Andrew made it out to be. He had other options he could have pursued vice withdrawing. Andrew undeniably lacked communications with his three forward companies and knew little of their status, but the Germans had ceased offensive actions with the onset of darkness. There was no German attack pressing him off his position on Point 107. One option open to Andrew was the employment of assets organic to 22 Battalion. Companies A and B were still intact and had only suffered minimum casualties during the early hours of the invasion. One or both of these companies could have been used to reinforce his forward companies or to conduct a counter-attack, but Andrew failed to utilize this option. Another option available involved reinforcements from Brigade Headquarters. Andrew knew reinforcements were on the way, even though he did not know when they would arrive. With these reinforcements it would have been possible for him to push patrols forward under the cover of darkness to discover the true state of affairs with C, D, and HQ Companies. He would have then been able to form a new tactical position on Point 107, maintain control of the airfield, and repulse any German attack in the morning. It is difficult to comprehend how withdrawing the battalion to B Company ridge would have improved his tactical situation except to aid in further withdrawal.[140] Even Creforce Headquarters could not understand why Andrew withdrew. Stewart, Freyberg's General Staff Officer, wrote afterwards, "It is difficult to justify in any way the Battalion Commander's decision to withdraw. If ever there was a case for the textbook expression, 'defense to the last man and the last round,' it was here."[141]

---

[140] Davin, 114 – 116.
[141] Singleton-Gates, 162.

One reason for Andrew's misgivings about 22 Battalion's situation was his failure to envision the battle from the enemy's perspective. Andrew was aware of how a German airborne attack would unfold due to a captured airborne manual. As noted earlier, he knew the number and type of units in the airborne organization along with the weapons, equipment and supplies that would accompany them.[142] Andrew witnessed the German invasion and estimated an enemy strength of approximately 400 men in and around 22 Battalion's area. He had no reason to believe any additional German forces were in his area. Andrew saw first hand the "duck shoot" his men participated in with the slow descending paratroops. He knew the fighting on the first day was intense but failed to comprehend the tactical strength of the defense and the disadvantage an enemy has when attacking a prepared position. If he had considered the effects of the long day of intense fighting on the invading German force, he may have chosen to remain on Point 107 and make a stand. The situation for 22 Battalion obviously looked bad in Andrew's eyes, but he should have realized the situation for the Germans was even worse. Many of the German officers were killed or wounded in the first few hours of fighting.[143] Although trained to operate in chaos, the German soldiers lacked any substantial organization to coordinate a large-scale attack.[144] More importantly, the German soldiers lacked ammunition. Student commented on the situation at Maleme, "If the enemy had made a united all-out effort in counter-attacking during that night from the 20th to the 21st or in the morning of the 21st, then the very tired remnants of the Assault Regiment suffering from lack of ammunition could have been wiped out."[145] Andrew was so close to victory but walked away from it.

---

[142] Westwood, 46; Donald interview.
[143] Heydte, 15.
[144] Heydte, 22.
[145] Singleton-Gates, 162.

GERMAN LEADERSHIP: GENERAL STUDENT

The German force invading Crete may have lacked men, weapons, equipment, and ammunition, but there was no lack of German leadership.[146] While Freyberg had little desire to remain on Crete and see to the defense of the island, Student had no other desire than to attack Crete and destroy the defenders.

The German plan to invade Crete was Student's own, personal plan, and his determined leadership was the driving factor behind the success of Operation MERCURY. Student devised the invasion plan, struggled against heavy opposition for its acceptance, and worked out its details. Colonel Baron von der Hydte, a battalion commander in Student's Assault Regiment, best sums up how the General viewed Operation MERCURY.

> General Student was obsessed by the idea of carrying out the tasks which had been assigned to him—or rather, which he had assigned to himself. The General, who to outward appearance was so calm and cool, was inwardly impelled by the passion of an explorer or inventor. It was therefore up to him to prove that it was possible to capture a defended island from the air with paratroops—an undertaking which no one had ever previously dared to attempt. He was consequently determined to show that there was no island which could not be taken from the air. In a certain sense, Crete was for him the great experiment which was to prove that his theory was right.[147]

It was this type of determination and conviction that was lacking in the Allied leadership for the defense of Crete. It was this type of leadership that meant the difference between success and failure.

Student's elite paratroops failed in their mission to secure the airfields during the first day of fighting, yet the General's resolve stood strong. Late in the evening of 20 May, Student ordered his only reserve paratroop units, two companies, to be dropped the next morning near Maleme where it appeared some success had been gained during the first day. During the morning of 21

---

[146] Heydte, 101.

May, unaware of any progress his forces may have had at the airfield, Student rolled the dice in a move that would either mean success or failure for the invading Germans. He ordered transport aircraft carrying elements of 5 Mountain Division to land at Maleme. Brave pilots followed their orders and landed at Maleme under heavy Allied artillery and machine gun fire. Mountain troops were now on Crete, but the cost was enormous. At the close of the second day of fighting scores of soldiers from the 5 Mountain Division lay dead on the airfield and some 80 damaged or destroyed aircraft littered the area around it.[148] Maleme airfield was now firmly in the hands of the Germans, but Student's battles were not over.

Crete was not Hitler's number one concern—Russia was. In keeping with Hitler's time table and anticipating Operation MERCURY being a quick victory, all German dive-bombers and transport aircraft were to be transferred from the Mediterranean theater to the Polish theater on 25 May in support of Operation BARBAROSA, the German invasion of Russia. Without dive-bombers and transports Student would be unable to re-supply his forces while the British Royal Navy would have unrestricted access to the island and be able to re-supply and reinforce Allied forces at will. Student fought a grueling battle with the German Army High Command to keep his aircraft. Air support continued on 26 May, but he lost dive-bomber support beginning on 27 May. The irony of this ordeal was that while Student's determined leadership was fighting for dive-bomber support, the Allied High Command in the Middle East had decided to evacuate Crete.[149]

---

[147] Heydte, 141.
[148] Schreiber 3, 547.
[149] Heydte, 140-142.

CONCLUSION

Operation MERCURY was an extremely bold plan. Hitler selected paratroops, his best trained and most highly prized soldiers, to undertake a mission that seemed almost suicidal. To send an airborne force to attack a well prepared enemy position, of which very little was known, with no means of re-supply or reinforcement until an enemy-held airfield was secured, was indeed a bold move and leans more towards the spectrum of a gamble vice a risk.

The use of Hitler's elite airborne units against a mix-match of hastily thrown together Allied forces was not the reason for German success on Crete. Allied troops were tenacious fighters and gave as good as they got. New Zealand soldiers and junior officers fought with heroic efforts to the very end. In fact, the casualties the German paratroops endured were so high Hitler was appalled and refused to use them in an airborne role for the remainder of the war.[150] The problem for the Allies did not reside in German paratroops but in Creforce leadership. ULTRA had given the Allies detailed knowledge of the impending German invasion. It warned specifically, accurately, and in detail about both an airborne and a seaborne landing.[151] However, "ULTRA was a shadow until the Generals gave it substance."[152] Every battle has a theme, and the theme for MERCURY was airfields—Freyberg misinterpreted this. Freyberg was not overly concerned about an airborne invasion but feared an invasion from the sea. Even with the Royal Navy dominating the seas, Freyberg still refused to move forces guarding the coastline to aid in the defense of the airfield at Maleme.[153] When Freyberg finally realized the consequence of the Germans gaining control of the Maleme airfield, it was too late.

---

[150] Schreiber 3, 553.
[151] Lewin, 158.
[152] Lewin, 159.
[153] Lewin, 158.

One must wonder about Freyberg's reluctance to assume command of the Allied forces on Crete. With all the effort he expended to avoid commanding Creforce, how much effort did he truly put into holding Crete at all costs, and how much of this reluctant attitude carried to his subordinate commanders? One needs look no further than to the officers in Freyberg's own New Zealand Division to find the answer. As critical as maintaining control of the airfields was to the Allied defense, Point 107 and its occupiers who controlled the Maleme airfield, was virtually handed to the Germans. Andrew's leadership comes into question when in the fog of war he loses communications with his forward units and subsequently forfeits his ability to fight his battalion as a unit. What conclusion was Andrew to draw from his superiors when he asked for help and none came? When Andrew was contemplating withdrawing, how much did Hargest's reply, "If you must, you must," effect his determination to hold his position and prevent the Germans from gaining control of the airfield?[154] It appears clear that the New Zealand leadership lacked the resolve and fortitude to defend Crete at all costs. The Germans did not win the battle for Crete by overwhelming Luftwaffe superiority, as Wavell reported.[155] New Zealand leaders, lacking determination and conviction, were not willing to "hold at all costs" a small island with men who had volunteered to leave their own country to fight a war on the other side of the world.[156]

Allied efforts against the Germans up to this point in the war had resulted in defeat, withdrawal, and evacuation. Freyberg was no stranger to this sequence of events. During World War I, Freyberg experienced defeat, withdrawal, and evacuation at Antwerp and Gallipoli.[157] In their first actions of World War II, Freyberg and the New Zealand Division experienced defeat,

---

[154] Davin, 110.
[155] Wavell, 3437.
[156] Singleton-Gates, 142.
[157] Singleton-Gates, 142-143.

withdrawal, and evacuation in Greece. Freyberg's first experience of battle in the Second World War brought back the horrors of Antwerp and Gallipoli and weighed heavy on his mind, "That sickening retreat, then stand and fight, then retreat again, with rearguards halting the German hordes, only themselves to retreat after a few hours."[158] Defeat, withdrawal, and evacuation became an acceptable course of action for the Allied leadership. This mind set was prevalent in the Creforce Commander as well as the subordinate commanders in the New Zealand Division.

Another overwhelming factor contributing to the defeat of the Allies was a lack of aggressive New Zealand leaders, poor communications and situational awareness, and a tendency for key direction to remain in command posts during critical periods of the battle instead of being forward where it could observe and influence the events. Stewart, Freyberg's General Staff Officer, commented about the action afterwards,

> A striking feature of the battle was a tendency for senior officers to stay in their headquarters. In subsequent campaigns it was the accepted practice in the Division for the commanders to be well forward...while the general staff officers remained at main headquarters. In Crete where communications were always bad and often non-existent, it was more important than ever that commanders should have gone forward. Had Brigadier Hargest...gone to his forward battalions himself instead of sending his Brigade Major there might be a different story to tell. Surely he would have vetoed the withdrawal...and his presence would have inspired his troops at a time when inspiration was needed."[159]

Stewart specifically mentions Hargest in this dispatch, but it should also be noted that the New Zealand Division Commander, Brigadier Edward Puttick, also remained in his CP during the Allies' final attempt to retake Maleme airfield the night of 21 May to the afternoon of 22 May.[160]

In July 1863, after the Confederate Army was defeated by the Union Army at the Battle of Gettysburg, General Robert E. Lee, Commanding Officer of the Army of Northern Virginia, stated that it was his fault the Confederate Army had been defeated and that the blame for the

---

[158] Singleton-Gates, 143.
[159] Singleton-Gates, 162.

defeat rested on him and him alone.[161] Similarly, Freyberg wrote after the battle for Crete, "I do not for one moment hold Colonel Andrew responsible for the failure to hold Maleme. I take full responsibility as regards holding the aerodrome."[162] This was easy for Freyberg to say, since he had already been successful at shifting the responsibility of defeat to higher headquarters and at making himself look like a hero by holding out on Crete for 10 days with seemingly inadequate resources and support against the mightiest warriors Germany could muster. The difference here is Lee, like Student, was dedicated to his cause and put 100 percent of his efforts into leading his men and winning the battle. Freyberg was indeed the Creforce Commander, but his dedication to the cause is left in question.

---

[160] Davin, 194.

[161] Jeffry D. Wert, *Gettysburg: Day Three* (New York: Simon and Schuster, 2001), 251.

[162] Singleton-Gates, 162.

BIBLIOGRAPHY

Butler, J.R.M. *Grand Strategy*. Vol. 2 of *History of the Second World War: September 1939 – June 1941*. London: Her Majesty's Stationary Office, 1957.

Churchill, Winston S. *The Grand Alliance: The Second World War*. Boston: Houghton Mifflin Co., 1950.

Cody, J.F. *21 Battalion: Official History of New Zealand in the Second World War 1939-45*. Wellington, New Zealand: Whitcombe and Tombs Ltd., 1958.

Davin, Daniel M. *Crete: Official History of New Zealand in the Second World War 1939 – 45*. London: Oxford University Press, 1953.

Donald, Haddon. Platoon Commander, 22 Battalion, 2nd New Zealand Division, 1941. Interview by Sergeant Brenton Beach, Army Museum, Waiouru, New Zealand, 18 August 2001. Cassette, 120 min.

Henderson, Jim. *22 Battalion: Official History of New Zealand in the Second World War 1939-45*. Wellington, New Zealand: Whitcombe and Tombs Ltd., 1958.

Heydte, Baron von der. *Deadalus Returned: Crete 1941*. Trans. W. Stanley Moss. London: Hutchinson and Co., 1958.

Hinsly, F.H. *British Intelligence in the Second World War*. New York: Cambridge University Press, 1993.

Lewin, Ronald. *Ultra Goes to War*. New York: McGraw Hill Book Company, 1978.

MacDonald, Callum. *The Battle of Crete*. New York: McMillan, 1993.

Montgomery, Bernard Law. *The Memoirs of Field-Marshall the Viscount Montgomory of Alamein, K.G.* Cleveland: The World Publishing Company, 1958.

Playfair, I.S.O., and others. *The Mediterranean and the Middle East*. Vol. 2 of *History of the Second World War: The Germans come to the Help of their Ally*. 2d imp. London: Her Majesty's Stationary Office, 1961.

Schreiber, Gerhard K., and others, ed. *The Mediterranean, South-east Europe, and North Africa 1939 – 1941*. Vol. 3 of *Germany and the Second World War: From Italy's declaration of non-belligerence to the entry of the United States into the war*. Trans. Dean S. McMurry, and others. New York: Oxford University Press, 1995.

Seibt, Conrad. *The Crete Operation*. Europe: Historical Division, Headquarters, United States Army, n.d.

Singleton-Gates, Peter. *General Lord Freyberg, V.C.: An Unofficial Biography*. London: Michael Joseph, 1963.

Stevens, W.G. *Freyberg, V.C.: The Man, 1939-1945*. Sydney: A.H. & A.W. Reed, 1965.

Strategy and Tactics of the Great Commanders of World War II and Their Battles. Greenwich, CT: Brompton Books Corp., 1990.

Twigg, Frank Noney. Intelligence Sergeant, 22 Battalion, 2nd New Zealand Division, 1941. Interview by Sergeant Brenton Beach, Army Museum, Waiouru, New Zealand, 11 July 2001. Cassette, 120 min.

U.S. Marine Corps Doctrinal Publication (MCDP) 1. *Warfighting*. Washington, DC: U.S. Marine Corps, 1997.

Veranov, Michael, ed. *The Third Reich at War*. New York: Galahad Books, 1999.

Wavell, Archibald P. "Operations in the Middle East; 7 February 1941, to 15 July 1941." *Supplement to The London Gazette*, 3 July 1946, 3423-3444.

Wert, Jeffry D. *Gettysburg: Day Three*. New York: Simon and Schuster, 2001.

www.ingramcontent.com/pod-product-compliance
Lightning Source LLC
Chambersburg PA
CBHW081524040426

42447CB00013B/3331